PENGUIN
SPECIALS

Penguin Specials fill a gap. Written by some of today's most exciting and insightful writers, they are short enough to be read in a single sitting — when you're stuck on a train; in your lunch hour; between dinner and bedtime. Specials can provide a thought-provoking opinion, a primer to bring you up to date, or a striking piece of fiction. They are concise, original and affordable.

To browse digital and print Penguin Specials titles, please refer to **www.penguin.com.au/penguinspecials**

Utzon and the Sydney Opera House

DARYL DELLORA

PENGUIN BOOKS

UK | USA | Canada | Ireland | Australia
India | New Zealand | South Africa | China

Penguin Books is part of the Penguin Random House group of companies
whose addresses can be found at global.penguinrandomhouse.com.

Penguin
Random House
Australia

Digital edition published by Penguin Group (Australia), 2013
This edition published by Penguin Group (Australia), 2013

Printed and bound in Australia by Griffin Press, an accredited
ISO AS/NZS 14001 Environmental Management Systems printer.

ISBN: 9780143570806

penguin.com.au

MIX
Paper from
responsible sources
FSC® C009448

CONTENTS

This book is dedicated to
Mrs Barbara J Hocking LLB LLM,
the intellectual architect of the Mabo Case

The Man

As a boy I first saw the Opera House from the Sydney Harbour Bridge and I wondered what it was and marvelled at the imagination that had conceived it. That was my first meeting with Jørn Utzon, as it is for everyone who sees the spectacular shells on Bennelong Point. The architect is present in every aspect of the exterior, every tile, every curve of concrete, every step on the concourse. The interior, though, tells a different story.

Decades later I met Utzon for a second time, through the precious reels of archival news film that survive from his nine years in Australia, from 1957 to 1966. They reveal the story of the Opera House from its conception to the tragedy of Utzon being forced from the project, before he could complete his glass walls or any of the interiors; he never returned to Australia and never saw the finished building. I scoured every reel of that footage and felt I came to know this tall charming Dane. His effervescent personality, his wit and his intellect were recorded on every frame with a kind of raw honesty only archival film can deliver.

Later still, in June 1998, I was in Denmark with a film crew making a documentary about Utzon for the ABC. October of that year was to be the twenty-fifth anniversary of the opening of the Opera House by Queen Elizabeth. With my co-writer and producer I'd spent two years developing a script, and during that time made several attempts to contact Utzon. He had not responded. Many on the multinational team of design architects who worked closely with him did agree to be interviewed, and one in particular, fellow Dane Mogens Prip-Buus, was encouraging of our project. He was in regular contact with Utzon and, having read our script, kept him fully informed of what we were doing.

We had come to Denmark hoping Utzon would agree to at least speak with us, if not be interviewed on camera, but were well aware of his reclusive reputation. Journalists contacted him on almost a daily basis and he invariably avoided them. It had been twenty-five years since the last Australian film crew, led by Peter Luck in 1973, interviewed Utzon. When a Danish filmmaker could not get the famous architect's attention, in desperation she turned up on his doorstep in tears. The celebrated Australian author Geraldine Brooks used a similar tactic.

But now, it seemed, he would meet with us. The concierge at our hotel in Copenhagen told us Utzon himself had called and asked to speak to us. The concierge had been rather taken aback. There are two countries in the world where Utzon is a household name, Denmark and Australia. We thought it must have been his son Kim who'd called, but no, the concierge assured us, it was 'the big man'. Utzon was certainly that; at six foot, four and a half inches he towered physically, but he was also big in other ways. It was rare indeed for him to contact a journalist or filmmaker and invite them to visit.

He told us to come to the Jullesbaekhus café, near a forest in the seaside village of Hellebaek, but he did not say if he would agree to be interviewed. We immediately loaded the film gear into the car and drove the fifty kilometres north. Arriving just before the stipulated time of 10.30 a.m., we found a table with a good view of the forest and sat down to wait. It was just my producer and I; we had asked the rest of the film crew to stay away in case their presence should inadvertently pressure Utzon in any way. It was an incongruous situation, like a scene from a Cold War spy novel – Utzon was supposedly just going to appear out of the forest. We had no address, no way of contacting him. Rather nervously, we watched and waited. The occasional car drove past but did not stop.

Then a figure did emerge from the forest. I recognised him immediately. A tall man with a distinctive way of walking. Silver hair, dark sunglasses and a navy-blue sailing jacket. He loped towards us, his spritely gait belying his eighty years. We went out to meet him and were greeted with a beaming smile and a wave.

Utzon was relaxed, even chatty. He immediately made it clear why he had asked to meet us. 'Where is the film crew?' he said. 'Let's do the interview.' He too had read our script; he seemed to know exactly what we were after and was happy to oblige. He felt it was the right time to stretch out a hand to the Australian people. It was, he said, like finally answering a letter that had long gone unanswered.

We returned to his house, a short drive from the café, and he introduced us to his wife Lis, who spoke perfect English and to whom he would frequently turn for the exact word when he could not think of it. It was here on the edge of the forest that we filmed the interview. The modest, single-storey brick house he'd designed was comfortable, simple and modernist, a quiet retreat for him and Lis now their three children were grown. He gave us all the time we needed and put no question off limits.

For the rest of that day, Utzon was our host. He took us to his favourite restaurant in Hellebaek, at the foot of the famous Kronborg castle, the setting for Shakespeare's *Hamlet*. He highlighted the similarities between the castle and the Sydney Opera House, both of which sat on the end of a promontory and were surrounded by sea. It was Utzon's desire that the Opera House, although a monumental form, would appear to float like clouds on Bennelong Point; Kronborg castle did this in a similarly beautiful way.

He walked with us through the forest of birch trees beside his house to a small lake. This place was a constant source of inspiration for him. In the midst of his work on the Opera House, he told me, he would sometimes bring his architectural team here, and in winter when the lake was frozen they used it as a gigantic drawing board, scratching out their plans on its surface. This beautiful natural environment was Utzon's muse; he'd devised a concept that he called additive architecture which was based on elemental forms in nature, from the veins of a single leaf to a forest. Back in his house overlooking the forest he described it to me:

> If you look out here you see a field with flowers, and small bushes, and small trees and big trees. They're all consisting of small elements. And if you take them off and put them up on a table, it's a number of elements and together they make this [pointing to the forest]. And in architecture you have floors, walls, you have windows, doors and you have a lot of materials. So when you select them, you must have in mind that they should make up a whole or an expression of some kind. So this is what you do when you work, and I do it more with elements than most architects.

It was a strange experience for me, having watched hours of the forty-year-old Utzon, to now sit with him in person all these decades later. The odd thing was that he seemed not to have changed at all. The same piercing intellect shone through, the same infectious humour; he was always upbeat, especially when talking about the Opera House project. It was as if the younger man I had met on film was there just under the skin of this eighty-year-old. Sitting in the lounge room with the light streaming in from his deck, he took off his blue jacket to reveal a distinctly Scandinavian yellow jumper underneath and launched into an excited discourse about his favourite building.

Judging from his home, the Sydney Opera House was never far from this thoughts, for dotted throughout were two-metre-square black and white photographs of the unfinished shells. Fixed on backing boards, they lent casually against the walls down the central corridor of the house. There was something impermanent about them, although they were images of a theatre that was built to stand for at least three hundred years.

Utzon talked about moving his whole family to Sydney in March 1963, once the shell construction was well under way. Lis, his daughter Lin and his two sons Jan and Kim all began a new life as Australians. He remembered the flight well. As the aircraft crossed the Pacific from Tahiti, he noticed some passengers being given socks to wear, and he requested five pairs for his family. 'Socks, sir, are only for first-class passengers,' he was brusquely informed. As they headed closer to Sydney the same hostess returned with a handful of socks, looking rather sheepish. It seemed there had been a radio message to the cockpit for Mr Utzon – from the Royal Yacht *Britannia*. Their Royal Majesties the Queen and the Duke of Edinburgh requested the pleasure of the company of Mr and Mrs Utzon for lunch.

On arrival at Sydney airport Jørn and Lis were immediately chauffeured off to meet the Queen, who was already two weeks into her second tour of Australia. It was an extraordinary way to begin their new life, to be taken directly from a long-haul flight to the saloon deck of the *Brittania*, anchored in Sydney Harbour. The assembled diners: on one side Her Majesty the Queen and the Duke, and on the other a motley crew of Olympic swimmers, businessmen and their wives, along with the author Patrick White (his partner Manoli was not invited), whose strident republicanism had not yet emerged. White thought Utzon certainly 'the most important guest' and 'as handsome as they come'.

Such a reception must have felt like a wonderful omen for the years to follow, but after this fairytale beginning reality soon struck home. Exhausted, Jørn and Lis picked up the children and drove to their hotel in Newport, on Sydney's northern beaches. Lin Utzon, then nearly seventeen years old, remembered vividly her first impressions of Sydney. After travelling halfway across the world through a host of exotic places, they had arrived, it seemed, back in a kind of quaint English county. The airport was small and rather ordinary, the houses all red brick, and the Newport Arms Hotel was little more than a run-down public bar with dozens of sweaty, singlet-clad men swilling beer – a bit different from the Royal Yacht.

Nevertheless the Utzons loved their time in Australia, and Jørn never forgot the kindness he was shown by ordinary people.

> It was a fabulous friendliness and we – as a family coming to Australia, as immigrants, when you compare what immigrants normally felt when they'd left their own country for a new country, and the problems they had with the language and with the work and so on, how terrible it can be – we were on the sunny side all the time. It was fabulous. We had so many friends afterwards, especially my wife and my children, because I didn't have so much time. We met this Australian openness which Australians don't know of themselves, because if

you've been in Europe and you come to any country in Europe, you'll feel a difference.

Lin Utzon adored Sydney and made many friends. To this day she describes it as the most beautiful of cities and regularly returns. Lis and Jørn told me their youngest boy Kim, then only six years old, was not so impressed. For a while he was scared to go to school. It seems his teacher had hit him, corporal punishment not being universally banned in New South Wales until 1997. But Sydney was to be their home and Utzon recounted the story of buying a block of land in Bayview, north of the city, high on the hill and overlooking the Pittwater inlet. He now regretted selling the block, which was worth little at the time. He had intended to build a family home there, and submitted plans for it to the local council. They were rejected, not an uncommon experience for Australians looking to build modernist houses back then, but Utzon was confident he would have got them through eventually.

What a different story might be told had he remained in Australia. The legacy of his unique work could have been dotted all over the nation. Instead we have only the one.

On that summer's day in the seaside village of Hellebaek, Jørn Utzon wanted to make one point above all others in respect of his time working on the Opera House: that his approach had been philosophical. He drew directly on many systems of thought, particularly those of the East, including Taoism, with its emphasis on simplicity, spontaneity, humility, and the importance of living in harmony with the natural world; and Confusianism, with its guiding principles of ethics, honesty and humanism. This thoughtful, reflective attitude governed Utzon's life and his approach to architecture.

The story of the Opera House, he stressed, was not simply a story about the architect, or the Minister for Public Works, who 'built it in another way'. The building had its own life now and he was grateful to have been a part of it. He had suffered so many indignities over the years but he did not wish to dwell on them. When the coalition government of New South Wales forced him out they refused even to supply a reference for him, and that alone had severely hampered his work prospects. But Utzon had pushed the bad times out of his mind, and was instead passionate and enthusiastic about the Opera House.

There was only one moment during that interview in 1998 when he nearly gave in to a despondency that must have pressed upon him many times since his departure from Sydney in 1966. I asked him if he thought the then Premier Robin Askin and his Minister Davis Hughes had actually understood his ideas all those years ago. Utzon paused for a moment and looked into the distance, moved uncomfortably in his seat and took a deep breath.

There was something happening I didn't know anything of. Davis Hughes had obviously his ideas and he would make this Opera House cheap and correct and he wanted more people in it and so on. And this is the authority of a Minister. An architect cannot do anything about it . . . He believed strongly in this. I think he, he is in love with that building. He finished it and he got a lot out of it. And the first time I met Mr Davis – I hope he will see the interview because I'm sure he'll remember it, he's still alive – he said that the story doesn't end before one of us dies! I'm still healthy!

Davis Hughes died in March 2003; he was ninety-two years old. Utzon sent a message of condolence to his widow, Philippa, which according to the *Sydney Morning Herald* left her in tears. 'Utzon must be a great man to have said what he did,' she was reported as saying. But Utzon's attitude had always been the same. He told me at Hellebaek in 1998:

It's not a story between us. It's actually a more or less normal architectural story, but he was taken with the Opera House, so when I came into his office the first time, he had two big easels on each side, with very big photographs of the Opera House site. So of course I thought this is the right man, he likes the Opera House. But obviously he wanted it in a different way. He was also, all the time afterwards, absorbed in it, in every detail. So it was his Opera House. He'd taken it over and he didn't want it to be like it was before, he wanted a different thing and so on. *Basta!*

This kind of magnanimous approach was typical of Utzon. He never felt compelled to drag down his critics. His focus was always on the job at hand. Unfortunately there were those who saw it as their mission to damage him, whether because of petty professional jealousy, or as a part of an opportunistic political ploy, or simply because they did not understand and could not accept this man and his exceptional artistic vision. There is an old adage that says a lie which is half true is ever the blackest of lies, because the element of truth in it gives weight to the falsehood. And so it was with the Opera House saga.

The First Myth

UTZON DID NOT KNOW HOW TO FINISH
THE SYDNEY OPERA HOUSE

This persisent, some would say scandalous,
myth about Jørn Utzon is best exemplified by
an unattributed quote dated February 1962:
'Lying on a beach in Hawaii, Utzon says to
Jack Zunz [deputy engineer on the project]
that he doesn't care if the Opera House is
never finished – he has already solved the
problems and can see a completed building in
his head.' Possibly the most damaging of all
the misinformation spread about Utzon, this
rumour first appeared in a calculated way
before his departure, in order to precipitate

it. After his departure it was repeated in order to justify his removal, and it has been perpetuated ever since, being quoted as recently as 2012 on an ABC website and in July 2013 on ABC Radio National.

Utzon, this rumour would have it, in the middle of one of the busiest times in the trajectory of the design and construction of the Sydney Opera House, while public servants, engineers, construction workers and labourers were hard at work on the project, was lying on a beach in Hawaii, of all places: weren't our beaches good enough for him? Perhaps he was taking a short holiday after working almost continuously on the project for the previous six years. Perhaps he was there to deliver a lecture to the Architecture Faculty of the University of Hawaii, where he later held a position. Perhaps he was on a brief stopover on the long flight from Hellebaek, where he and the other design architects were based at that time, via London where he had meetings with the engineers.

In truth Utzon never was in Hawaii in

February 1962. In January and February of that year he was in Denmark and London, returning to Sydney in mid-March, slightly later than planned due to delays caused by the Opera House engineers failing to submit their plans on time.

As for the second part of this rumour, that Utzon 'doesn't care if the Opera House is never finished', this would be an extraordinary thing for any architect to say, let alone one in the middle of the creation of one of the greatest public buildings the world has ever seen, and it would have been completely out of character for Utzon to behave in this way. His six years of work had been done painstakingly and with great dedication; the project was his magnum opus. And the conclusion, that Utzon 'has already solved the problems and can see a completed building in his head', made him sound like a dreamer, with no practical ability, just a bunch of extravagant imaginings that could never be realised. Sensible 'adults' like Liberal Premier Sir Robin Askin (the same premier who allegedly took big brown paper bags full of cash from his police commissioner) would have to come in and fix it all up.

Utzon did frequently make grand, almost poetic statements that reflected his vision, and these were easily taken out of context and debased. In June 1998 Utzon likened his method of working to that of the great master architects who had come before him. Like Antonio Gaudi, the famous Spanish architect of the unfinished Sagrada Familia Basilica in Barcelona, he was not concerned simply with getting the job done, but was focused on doing it in the best way possible.

So it was like visiting Gaudi's church in Barcelona. I went down and they were still working on this and I asked one of the good stone masons, 'When do you finish?' And he said, 'We don't know, we build!' And then I asked in Palma Majorca – where the cathedral was built in 12 hundred and something – I asked the guide, 'When did they finish this?' And he said, 'It's not finished yet.' [Pointing upwards] 'Up there, there's some windows that aren't finished yet.' [Laughing] More or less we had the feeling that we were just working on [the Opera House], and I think also there was this respect from the client's side that we had got the money, we had no problems with the money, the Opera House lottery gave us the money. So it was absolutely exceptional.

To suggest that Utzon did not know how to finish the Opera House is to misunderstand him and his methods. He was always striving for perfection, and if a search for perfection drives your artistic practice then you're never finished. This is a quite different notion from the simplistic one that he did not know *how* to finish. Indeed, Utzon's work on the Opera House never ceased. His daughter Lin Utzon told me in 2013 that her father thought about the building every day of his life, right up until his death in November 2008.

A lot has been written about Utzon's

eclecticism. He took ideas from a wide range of sources, cementing his concept of additive architecture. He looked to the Mayan temples as inspiration for his podium at the Opera House; he drew on the ancient Chinese building code, where every detail has its place. For the shape and construction of the external shells, he borrowed from the Arabic mosques with their tiled exteriors, and he even returned to the naval shipyards in his home town for their practical building methods based on model construction. It is not surprising, then, that he should talk in artistic and philosophical terms when discussing the guiding principles of his work, but any architect knows that in order to complete a work, especially a monumental one, they must have the full concept for it worked out in their head. No architect of Utzon's calibre begins work on such a project without any idea of where it might lead. It is at the point when they have the entire building in their head – and this might come early in the design process or late; for Utzon it appears to have been some time between 1962 and 1963 – that they can proceed to physically realise it.

Two other people, along with Utzon, are responsible for the Sydney Opera House as it stands today: Labor Premier Joe Cahill, who began the project and championed it, and Liberal Premier Robin Askin, who saw the political opportunity in damning it. Without Cahill, nothing like Utzon's grand vision would ever have been built, and indeed no opera house might have been realised in Australia for many years. Utzon was strongly of the view that no other country in the world at that time, certainly nowhere in Europe, would have commissioned his design.

John Joseph Cahill was an old-school Labor politician. Irish Catholic, he managed the impossible: he held the New South Wales Labor Party together when the federal and Victorian parties split over communism, leaving them both out of office for decades. Federal Labor remained in the wilderness from 1949 until Gough Whitlam led them back in 1972. In Victoria it was even longer, with Labor out of office for twenty-seven years until 1982. It takes a special sort of hard-headed politician to stay in power at the worst of times, and Cahill was at the heart of a continuous reign of New South Wales Labor for almost a quarter of a century.

When Utzon first met Cahill he queried the operation of the waterfront docks on Bennelong Point. It seems unthinkable now, but the original plan for the site allowed for cargo ships to continue to be loaded and unloaded right next to the Opera House. Cahill picked up the phone, rang the port authority, and had the Bennelong Point docks closed down there and then. It was immediately clear to Utzon that he and the premier shared a common vision, and the two men got on famously.

Utzon described Cahill's straightforward attitude to the Opera House to me:

[Premier Cahill] said we want this building because many people in this town, have shown that they want expressions like opera, theatre, and music in the same way as they have in big cities in Europe. And he said, 'I do not want my people to miss anything that they could get in Europe.' It was that simple and nice and marvellous.

Unfortunately for Utzon, Cahill died only three years into the project, in October 1959. From that point on the political situation in New South Wales was precarious, and for Utzon it became perilous. Without a powerful figure like Cahill to guide the project through, problems began to mount up. Joe Cahill, though, had made a brilliant decision only months before his death, and that was to begin construction of the foundations of the building. Until work had actually begun on the site there was always the possibility that a new administration, Labor or Liberal, would cancel the whole project: Cahill saw to it that this would never occur. No working design yet existed for the building itself, but with the tram sheds that had occupied the site now gone and tons of concrete poured in to support the new structure, there could be no turning back.

This decision, while it may have been a political masterstroke, later caused engineering and construction problems, since the foundations were poured at a time when nobody knew precisely what the final building would look like. It was three years before Utzon came up with his final scheme for the shells, and the foundations subsequently required major modification in order to hold up the structures. Paradoxically, while Cahill's decision ensured that the building of the Opera House would go ahead, it also sowed the seeds in the minds of some that Utzon had no idea how to finish the project.

As early as 1957, as a Liberal MLA, Robin Askin asked parliament if it was the right time to build this 'lavish venture'. Askin was testing the waters rather than outrightly condemning the project. He knew Premier

Cahill had already met with resistance in Labor circles when he first announced the international competition in 1955. Some felt it was hard to justify the huge expense involved, which could, perhaps, be better spent on housing, health and education.

As the years went by, Askin stepped up his attack. By 1959 he was Opposition leader. By 1962 he was moving amendments to the legislation that governed the funding of the project in order to highlight the cost 'over-runs'. This was certainly unfair, since no meaningful prediction of total costs had or could be produced at that stage. Whatever they might say, no politician or bureaucrat knew how much the Opera House would finally cost, because nothing like it had ever been built before and it was still very much a work in progress. Cahill had established the New South Wales Opera House Lottery in 1957, before any construction had commenced, and the income from the lottery would eventually pay for the entire cost of the building, so strictly speaking no taxpayer funds were being called upon. Nevertheless Askin's line of attack was enormously fruitful, and in 1965 he exploited it as an election issue.

Robin Askin ran a potent campaign using, among other things, the slogan 'fix up the Opera House mess'. Early on, the government had rather ineptly brought in a quantity surveyor with no experience whatsoever in this type of project to make an estimate of the total cost and time required for completion. The surveyor's woeful underestimate, of £3.5 million and about five years, had given Askin fuel for years of claims of mismanagement. Now the tabloid media ran saturation stories about the cost of the building, the budget over-runs, the time delays and, of course, stories on Utzon himself. Why did we need this foreigner? Surely Australian architects could do it better and quicker? The dog whistle of xenophobia wasn't far below the surface of what was essentially a parochial bid for office, and it was successful: Askin and the Liberal–Country Party coalition steamed into government in May 1965.

Unfortunately, as with all simplistic political promises, it was not so easy to do the 'fixing up'. There was no other building in the world that remotely resembled Utzon's Opera House. It was to be a monument, a national treasure. No part of it was easy, no part was cheap, and nobody could ever accurately put a timeframe on completion of the building work. There was no such thing as a quick fix.

In 1956 architects from all over the world had put in submissions to the competition to design an opera house for Sydney. Jørn Utzon's entry was number 218. His first move, after reading the competition brief, was to get hold of the sea charts of Sydney Harbour.

> We heard from an English magazine, an architectural magazine, it was not announced in Denmark, that there was such a job and

I immediately went to the shop where you can buy sea charts, and got one for Sydney Harbour, where you see the silhouette of the Heads and you see Bennelong Point, seen from the sea. And I thought this is what I want to participate in because it's marvellous . . . I looked at the Heads in Sydney and I thought a movement, a slow movement by people up hill where they somehow see the sky and the heads and then suddenly come up and see the sea and the whole horizon. This procession I liked very much. I like processions very much. And then I had in mind my visit to Mexico where they had built enormous platforms in the jungle, 8 metres high, 100 by 80 metres. On top of them they've put their temples because they wanted to come up somehow into a different world . . . And here the trick was actually to get people up – when you come up the steps you see no buildings, you see the sky and the shells . . . You get to another world, and that's what you want for your audience, to start already to separate themselves from their daily lives.

The world of architecture in the 1950s was divided along geographic and cultural lines. There was the American/British (and therefore Australian) approach and there was the European approach. The former was more hard and fast, adhering strictly to deadlines, schedules and budgets, but the European approach, especially on a project of grand national and cultural significance, was more free-flowing. Some of the most interesting work was being done by architects who crossed that divide: Sydney wunderkind Harry Seidler, for example, a Jewish refugee from Hilter's Austria; in the US, people like the founder of the Bauhaus, Walter Gropius; and Hungarian-born Marcel Breuer and Finnish American Eero Saarinen. Seidler and Saarinen had both noted and appreciated Utzon's work before he entered the Opera House competition.

On his arrival in Sydney Utzon made an immediate and lasting impression. He was an instant celebrity; everybody wanted to get close to this tall handsome Dane. This in itself caused problems: Utzon's own celebrity bored him. He preferred to concentrate on the architectural job at hand and did not always turn up to the dinners and balls arranged in his honour. As a result, certain wealthy and influential people in Sydney thought he did not show enough deference to them. On the other hand his relationships with the Labor government – particularly Cahill and the Minister for Public Works, Norm Ryan – and the Opera House Committee that oversaw the project, were excellent.

Even late in the piece, when Utzon was struggling with the bureaucrats in the Public Works Department over his plywood interiors, he remained close to Norm Ryan. The two men would inspect work at Ralph Symonds' plywood factory at Homebush Bay, or on site at Bennelong Point, and Ryan always showed enormous confidence in Utzon's ideas and his practicality. For his part Utzon would forever be grateful for Ryan's support for the first eight years of exciting work. Utzon fondly remembered:

I took him round to all these places, and he saw the mockups of the cladding, and the models in Ralph Symonds' factory. And there's a photograph of him and I in front of the shells. We're looking like two crooks almost, or happy boys, because we got away with something. And I had said shortly after to him, when we were parting, 'Norm, now you know everything about the Opera House.' 'No,' he said, 'Jørn, I know nothing, but you – you know everything and that's what matters.' Could I get a better feeling from my client, after eight years work with him?

But when Robin Askin began his decade-long domination of New South Wales, Norm Ryan could no longer help his Danish friend. Utzon never stood a chance against the dissembling of Askin and his Minister for Public Works, Davis Hughes. Askin was no aesthete, and later became infamous for his reported cry of 'Run the bastards over' when anti-Vietnam War protestors attempted to block the passage of visiting US President Johnson's motorcade.

Hughes, for his part, was notorious as a man who played fast and loose with the truth. Elected leader of the New South Wales Country Party in the 1950s, he had suddenly withdrawn from public view right before a state election campaign. A kind interpretation of this is that he suffered a nervous breakdown after the Labor Party revealed he had misrepresented himself on the parliamentary register. Hughes had signed on as a New South Wales MLA claiming he held a science degree from the University of Tasmania; in fact, he had never completed his studies. The Labor Party also pointed out that during the Second World War, Hughes had gained automatic advancement as an officer in the RAAF by claiming to have a bachelor of science.

Following his appointment as Minister, Davis Hughes' plan for the Opera House was a brutal one: he simply stopped making payments to the architect. For nine months he slowly strangled the project, until Utzon finally succumbed. Far from running out of ideas, Utzon was starved of funds. Although the Department of Public Works had often been tardy, they always paid eventually – until the election of the Askin government in May 1965. Thereafter Hughes stopped paying Utzon's running costs, and by February 1966 the architect was personally owed $300,000 by the government.

At this point, unable to run his office or pay his staff, Utzon wrote to Hughes:

Dear Minister,

In the meeting between yourself and Mr Wheatland and me today, you stated that you still could not accept my fee claim of £51,000 for Stage Technique, which I have requested from you for the past several months and which is completely justified.

I had been forced to set the 15th February, 1966, as the final date for receipt of this payment, and as you could not, at this date, 28th February, 1966, satisfy me on this, you have forced me to leave the job.

As I explained to you and as you know also from meetings and discussions, there has been no collaboration on the most vital items on the job in the last many months from your Department's side, and this also forces me to leave the job as I see clearly that you do not respect me as the architect.

Hughes and Askin jumped on Utzon's letter, which nowhere mentioned the word 'resignation', and treated it as just that. Whether Utzon imagined his letter was a resignation or not made no difference; Hughes and Askin would not budge. Utzon knew that no one else could successfully finish the project according to his vision, and he therefore thought that the government would have to ask him back. He could not have been more wrong. It appears it had been their intention all along to force him to resign, something made evident during the election campaign nine months earlier, with reports from Hughes' electorate (Armidale) of him saying he would get rid of Utzon. Having now achieved that aim, he and Askin no doubt enjoyed a good laugh at the notion that the architect, after writing his own resignation letter, now thought they would reinstate him.

Next Utzon, rather tragically, entered into a series of negotiations with Askin and Hughes, attempting to find a compromise that would allow him to continue. Their proposal was that Utzon be returned as 'design architect', under the supervision of the Government Architects office. He would be allowed to make design suggestions but another architect would make the final decisions. This was the ultimate humiliation for Utzon, and he could never have accepted such a demotion; moreover there is little to suggest the proposition was even made in good faith, since it would have been entirely unworkable. His solution to the complex problem of the construction of the Opera House shells, for one, would never have been implemented under such an arrangement.

When it was clear that Utzon was not going to return to the project, there were public demonstrations against the government. A letter from dozens of the world's leading architects was sent to Askin demanding Utzon's reinstatement, but it was all to no avail.

Davis Hughes put a new architectural team in charge. This was led by design architect Peter Hall, who literally had no idea what was required. Hall had designed a few New South Wales University buildings quite competently – dark brick, dark corridors, linoleum floors – all finished on time and well within budget. He had won awards and was certainly in the top tier in the New South Wales Government Architect's office, but he was no Jørn Utzon. Hall seriously contemplated resignation himself only a few weeks into his appointment, once he realised the true scale of the project and the techincal issues Utzon had been grappling with. Most buildings, and certainly all those that Peter Hall had previously designed, have a rectilinear geometry. The curvilinear nature of Utzon's shells threw up an array of challenging problems for the interior design.

But for Hughes to lose his replacement architect so early in the piece would have been politically disastrous, so he offered Hall and his wife an all-expenses-paid world tour to help him reconsider. Hall took the trip and stayed on. During these three months, with Hall travelling the world courtesy of the New South Wales government, no work was done on the Opera House. When Hall did finally begin, he embarked on an exercise akin to re-inventing the wheel. He and his team went through all the schematic drawings and sketches and models Utzon had left behind, and tried to imagine what he might have been going to do next. Hall's engagement with Utzon's ideas was at a very superficial level. Those ideas provided an obvious initial inspiration for the Australian replacement, but after that he was on his own.

On returning to Denmark, Utzon had left many preliminary drawings and some models for the interiors and the glass walls of the Opera House. Full working drawings – that is, the step that takes design ideas into concrete buildable forms – did not exist, since the preparation of these were at the heart of the standoff between Utzon and Hughes. To complete the working drawings, Utzon needed funds to build mock-ups and test his ideas; Hughes simply demanded to see the drawings before he would authorise any payments. This was a calculated decision on Hughes' part, intended to stymie Utzon, since it was clear that the building of models had been integral to every stage of Utzon's work to this point. The solution for the shells would never have emerged if he had not been able to build models.

In his resulting legal dispute with the New South Wales government over his unpaid fees, which amounted to a breach of contract, Utzon was represented by a young Neville Wran QC, the future Labor Premier. The matter was not resolved until nearly forty years later, when Labor Premier Bob Carr agreed to pay Utzon, at his request, the symbolic fee of $300,000 – by then amounting to far less than he was owed in real terms – to accept the position of consulting architect to the Opera House.

By the time Utzon left Australia the vast concrete shells of the exterior were virtually finished, but they were open-ended structures with no interiors and none of the glass walls that would enclose each end of each shell. Utzon's scheme for these walls was based on the subtle unfurling of the wing of a bird. Each piece of glass was to be housed in plywood mullions, each would be prefabricated and then put together on-site, and there were to be a minimal number of different shapes and sizes of glass.

Peter Hall took a completely different approach. His glass walls, rather than draping down like a curtain, jutted out almost horizontally. Little of the nuanced and delicate effect of Utzon's ideas remained; his guiding philosophy of additive architecture was nowhere to be seen on the inside of the building. Hall proudly boasted that every one of the hundreds of pieces of glass in his walls had to be cut to a unique shape and size, all determined by a computer program – and as a result enormously expensive and time-consuming.

Utzon claimed that, had he remained in Australia, he would have finished the building within eighteen months. He had already worked on the project for nine years, solving the most difficult of problems – how to build the shells. It seems hard to believe that the interiors, no less important but far less demanding, would have taken him almost as long again, which was what they took. It's important to remember that for the first three of those nine years, no building work had begun. In addition, when he left the project many of his ideas for the interiors were well in hand, drawings existed, and some models had already been built and tested by plywood manufacturer Ralph Symons (although this was done at Symons' expense and did not come close to the volume of work needed for Utzon to fully test his ideas). The new architectural team began on the interiors from scratch, since Hall, after taking inspiration from Utzon, developed his own quite different approach.

The six years of building work under Utzon cost $22 million. The new team worked for nearly eight more years and spent a staggering $80 million. If Utzon had continued in the job, spending at the same rate and finishing in the timeframe he gave, the total cost would have been $52 million instead of the actual $102 million. Askin had complained bitterly about the cost of the project while in opposition, and then once in government spent at a rate conservatively estimated to be 96 per cent more than the previous government.

The truth is there was no 'mess' at the Sydney Opera House under Utzon. There had been many problems, that is true, but in every case they had been solved with original and exciting architectural ideas. There was no reason why Utzon's successful approach could not have continued to completion. The Australian architectural profession was united on this point, almost to a man (there were few women; as late as 2004 only one per cent of directors of Australian architecture firms were women). Even Peter Hall himself had been one of the first to sign the petition calling for Utzon's reinstatement – but that was before he decided to accept the job as his replacement.

The fact that in the end, the interiors and the glass walls that enclose the shells were vastly inferior to the magnificence of Utzon's plans for them was due not only to Hall being unable to match Utzon's design brilliance, but also to changes demanded by the government in the seating and basic functions of each hall. It's this that gave rise to the standing joke, 'Australia has the best opera house in the world – the exterior is in Sydney and the interior is in Melbourne.'

One of the most damaging acts of the government and the Opera House Committee after Utzon's departure was to dramatically change the brief he had been given. The major hall, which under the original brief was to be dual-purpose, both a concert hall for symphony orchestra and an opera theatre, was changed to accommodate only the former. At the same time the number of seats in it were increased. Opera was shunted off to the minor hall, which was originally intended for drama only, because in the mid-1960s fewer people in Sydney attended the opera than attended symphony orchestra performances. Even though it was an *opera house* that was being built on Bennelong Point, the government decided, with no forward thinking at all, to put greater emphasis on the concert hall, to the detriment of opera. Askin, Hughes and Opera House Committee heavyweight Sir Charles Moses, the revered head of the ABC, could not imagine a time, less than a decade later, when audiences would come in numbers to the greatest opera house in the world to see – opera.

The problems with the interiors of the Sydney Opera House, which derive from the government's changed brief and the new architect's inability to deal with it, are so grave and numerous that it is impossible to list them here. It is enough to say that no grand opera, such as Verdi's *Aida*, can be properly staged in the concert hall (the major hall) because it has no staging gear. Nor can such operas be staged in the opera theatre itself (the minor hall), because it's too small. In a tragic metaphor for where the whole project ended up, the staging gear, brought at massive expense from Austria, was removed after Utzon's departure and sent to Long Bay Prison for inmates to cut up as scrap metal. Utzon told me that the demolition expert who removed the gear was distraught, saying 'it was like cutting up a live deer'. Moreover the minor hall can only accommodate ballet by putting the dancers at risk. Performers are forced to run off into wings that barely exist, and as a result injuries have been common. The inadequate dimensions of the orchestra pit have led to musicians suffering hearing loss and have severely compromised the acoustics of the hall.

The acoustics of the major hall are also inferior, despite many ad hoc fix-ups, including, early on, the installation of eighteen huge acrylic ceiling rings designed to reflect sound back onto the stage so that the orchestra can hear itself perform. It has been a sad and fruitless effort to improve the delivery of the one thing the project was meant to be all about – fine music.

There is one final nail in the coffin of the idea that Jørn Utzon did not know how to finish the Sydney Opera House and so resigned: the Kuwait National Assembly Building. Utzon designed this monumental work after once more winning an international competition, in 1971. Anyone who has seen its massive curved concrete forms, reminiscent of Le Corbusier's famous High Court Building in Chandigarh, India, immediately recognises it as no less impressive and certainly no less complex than the Sydney Opera House itself. Building work began on it in 1978 and was finished in 1982, and the whole building conformed to Utzon's philosophy of additive architecture.

The Second Myth

THE INTERIORS UTZON DESIGNED WERE
NOT CAPABLE OF BEING BUILT

The interiors of the Sydney Opera House
(the glass walls that enclose the shells, and
all the architectural detailing that goes with
them, especially the acoustic elements) was
stage three of the project. Stage one was the
podium and foundations. Stage two was the
building of the shells, undoubtedly the most
innovative and complex phase. Utzon's concept for the interiors can only be understood
in relation to his concept for the shells. The
two are inextricably linked, relying on each
other for function and meaning.

His original, competition-winning design was for a streamlined concrete shell structure that was lower than the one eventually built. The most famous of the buildings of the late 1950s and early 1960s that employed lightweight concrete shells is Eero Saarinen's TWA airport terminal in New York, begun in 1956. Utzon was certainly inspired by this building, beginning his design for the Opera House at roughly the same time. It is not surprising, then, that Opera House competition judge Eero Saarinen immediately took to Utzon's concept.

In the end, though, the building on Bennelong Point was not really a shell structure at all. Concrete shell structures are beautiful, sensuous forms but they must, as a simple matter of physics, remain relatively low in profile. Utzon's shells were directly inspired by the churches of the gothic period; he liked the connection to these extraordinary places of worship, and felt that audiences would come to the Opera House in a similarly reverential way. But the

Sydney Opera House required a structure that soared up even higher, sixty-five metres at one end, to encompass stage gear, and a concrete shell structure was physically incapable of supporting the weight of such a height. This posed the conundrum of what kind of form should be employed for the shells. Should it be an ellipsoid? A parabola? A catenary?

Work on this difficult mathematical problem took up thousands of hours of the engineers' time and expertise – a staggering 150,000 hours by February 1962 – and yet after two years they were no closer to resolution. Finally Utzon solved the problem himself; with a unique mix of aesthetics and mathematics, he developed his famous 'spherical solution'.

At its simplest, this meant that every element in each of the shells would be taken from a sphere of the same radius. It followed that the manufacture of these elements could then be done uniformly and cheaply. The spherical solution also carried with it the solution to another perplexing issue, the question of the shape of the tiles that were to cover the shells. Once the curvature of the shells was determined to be spherical, it followed as rudimentary geometry that the tiles should be square.

The engineering firm attached to the project was the distinguished British group Ove Arup & Partners. Ove Arup himself was of Danish extraction and had notable experience in lightweight reinforced concrete construction. Initially Utzon and Arup formed a close friendship, but by 1962 cracks had appeared. Arup was furious when Utzon's breakthrough perfunctorily dispensed with the concrete shell approach and, understandably, he felt cheated. He had undertaken a huge amount of work, in good faith, attempting to solve the problem. Utzon's answer, as he saw it, was to a slightly different question. What had begun as a very constructive and creative partnership between architect and engineers was now increasingly under strain. To make matters worse, the firm of engineers was close to financial collapse and their leader chronically ill.

Nevertheless, to his credit, Arup, who understood Utzon and his vision for the Opera House, stated unequivocally that only if the architect was 'given his head' could the building be the world's 'foremost contemporary masterpiece'. That firmly held view was at the heart of Arup's decision to invest so much in the building, personally as well as financially. Ove Arup took Utzon's spherical solution and refined it, helping to create the extraordinary structures that exist today. There is no doubt that it was a unique relationship between architects and engineers, but it is quite wrong to say, as some engineering texts do to this day, that Ove Arup & Partners were the architects of the Sydney Opera House. Or that deputy engineer Jack Zunz (the man on the beach in Hawaii) designed the shells. Zunz was the principal *structural* designer, and no doubt without him the project would have suffered enormously, but it was Jørn Utzon who formulated the design concept.

By 1962, with the entire scheme for the shells complete, construction of the two halls and the restaurant could now proceed apace. As this second stage drew to a close, the role of the engineers should, under normal circumstances, have moved into the background, allowing the architect to really come into his own in stage three. But in an unusual contractual arrangement, for stages one and two both the engineers and the architects dealt directly with the client, the New South Wales government, on an equal footing. This caused problems: the normal chain of command in the industry was for engineers to answer to the architects, and the architects to the client. Even the Royal Australian Institute of Architects – whose support for Utzon was at times equivocal – complained about the precedent this contract set. With the equal-footing arrangement, the engineers began to second-guess Utzon's plans and even to suggest alternative architectural approaches. Michael Lewis, Ove Arup & Partners' site manager on Bennelong Point and deputy to Jack Zunz, made no bones about what he thought of Utzon's concept:

> The site is quite unsuited for the purpose. It's a marvellous site, it's wonderful; the water's all round it, the harbour's beautiful and everything's excellent but to get people there and to use it as a cultural centre is really quite wrong. So you start off with the wrong site and then you select a scheme which defies a few fundamental principles, like they don't know quite how the roof is going to work, they don't know quite how the stage machinery is going to work and you put these two halls side by side.

As the months passed, Utzon and the engineers began to move further and further apart. Suspicions and recriminations were never far from the surface, exacerbated by the unusual contractual arrangement with the state government and not helped by the humiliation, both financial and professional, of the engineers' failed attempts to make

Utzon's original concrete shell concept work. The last straw came when the engineers, without Utzon's input, prepared a report for government suggesting that his concepts for the interiors could not be built. Utzon had recommended Ove Arup for the job at the very start. The two men had become close friends. Now Utzon felt that he had been betrayed by Arup's firm.

Every element in Utzon's Opera House was designed to be in harmony with every other element. This was the case for the interiors as well, which he intended to be as exciting and compelling as the exterior. Utzon described the building as being like a walnut, having a hard, smooth exterior shell which, on opening, surprises with the unexpected shape of its kernel. But the two, exterior and interior, always remain in complete harmony. His plan was for the underside of the vaulting roofs to be left exposed, visible from the inside. When patrons entered they would first see the interior of the concrete shells; the eye would then be drawn to the soaring vaults, the lines and the ribs of their beams all soaring upwards. It was only after taking in the splendour of these awe-inspiring shapes that the second part of the interiors, the plywood boxes comprising the ceiling and the walls of the auditorium, would be apparent. This plywood form would sit as an almost autonomous structure, nestled within the first like the kernel of the walnut.

Utzon's kernel was to be constructed entirely from huge curved sheets of plywood made by Ralph Symons's company, which had developed specialised techniques that no other manufacturer could duplicate. Symons had built train carriages that required continuous lengths of fifteen metres or more; most spectacularly, he'd provided the enormous curved sheets for Melbourne's Sidney Myer Music Bowl. Utzon wanted to use these sheets as structural elements in their own right, rather than simply cladding over steel. His design called for long plywood boxes that would radiate out from the stage. Their rectangular shape would add to the structural stability and also offer an elegant way to house the air conditioning, lighting and electricity. Part of the structural support for these boxes would also come from the concrete shells themselves, and it was this aspect that Ove Arup & Partners frowned upon. The engineers' report suggested that the plywood would be too heavy to be fully supported by the shells and, equally, would not be strong enough to be self-supporting. Their alternative was cheaper, quicker and easier to build but it did not allow for the autonomous acoustic kernel of Utzon's concept, and he feared the acoustic quality would be poorer as a result. On that score he was certainly right.

Utzon was convinced that his dual approach was feasible: the two structural supports would spread the load. He received a second opinion from Peter Miller, of the respected Sydney firm of consulting engineers, Milston & Ferris. Miller strongly disagreed with the assessment made by Ove Arup & Partners, reporting: 'There seems [to be] no reason why the whole ceiling should not be pre-fabricated and pre-finished. The erection procedures proposed would be relatively simple . . .' Utzon became convinced that the engineers were against him and the relationship grew poisonous, with both sides fearing that the other was conspiring to remove them from the project. In the end, of course, it was Utzon who was removed, but there was no technical reason why his interiors were not built, only a human one, with the lack of a suitable compromise.

The final ingredient in Utzon's plan for the interiors was a breathtaking use of colour. After travelling to Queensland's Great Barrier Reef and seeing how the bright, reflective surface of the water gave way to a kaleidoscope of tropical colour when he dived beneath, he wanted a similar experience for theatregoers. The stunning white exterior of the Opera House, surrounded by glistening water on Bennelong Point, would give way to something quite different and quite spectacular.

The colours from the fish on the reef I liked very much, and then of course you see on the outside, if it's white on the outside, and then silver and then perhaps yellow on the inside, and gold and red, on the inside. But then the light would come in from the windows between the shells, and fall on the shapes of the halls. And you could see the light coming down and feel that hall was separated from the shells, like a walnut, inside the shell.

Radiating lines of colour would focus the eye on the stage, and then, as the houselights dimmed, it would be the performance that took over. Utzon had calculated all these variables precisely. He had planned each step of his audience in their procession from the dreary and the humdrum to a higher level, through the dramatic vaulting space to an unexpected world of vibrant colour: red, silver, yellow and gold.

Every single element in the scheme had its own special place. He had even begun planning for large-scale artworks on the walls. The most famous architect of the day, Le Corbusier, was fascinated when Utzon described his ideas to him – the notion of a procession, the foyer with its vaulting roof, followed by a huge tapestry or painting. Hearing this, Le Corbusier responded excitedly to Utzon, 'Ah! You are an architect!'

But Australia, and the world, was denied the genius of Utzon's ideas for the interiors and the glass walls, because Davis Hughes claimed to know better – better than the architect of a building now universally hailed as a modern masterpiece. It was a triumph of base politics over art. The greatness of the building that now stands on Bennelong Point does not derive from the interiors designed by Peter Hall.

Nevertheless, while Utzon was alive he never uttered a word against the designs that the new architectural team put in place. He accepted the building as it was, an expression of its time, and again it was his philosophical approach to architecture that came to the fore when I spoke with him in 1998.

> I don't think it's good for me or for you to go deep into a discussion of what would've been, when we have a building of that magnitude, so marvellous, which functions so good, and Peter Hall and his people worked on it with a respect for it, plus they had a job to do from the new planning authority. And people like it; I'm not a fellow who wants to go around and criticise when I've been in this, and also the day we left Australia, I didn't leave because I'd made errors, or because it was too expensive, I left because new authority didn't want me. So I was not happy, but I was not unhappy about something I couldn't do. Again, *basta!*

The week after our documentary film *The Edge of the Possible* screened nationally on the ABC in October 1998, Premier Bob Carr wrote to Utzon and asked him to accept the position of consulting architect.

Utzon was very pleased to do so: the reply to the long-unanswered letter from Australia would now truly be mailed. Remaining in Europe during the process, he prepared a set of design principles while his son Jan, also an architect, travelled to Australia to liaise with the government and the Opera House. Since then, many details of the building have been refurbished, with Utzon's collaboration.

The interior of the smallest space in the complex, which seats two hundred people, has been renovated according to Utzon's original vision and is now called the Utzon Room. It is used regularly for public and corporate events. Colour has finally been incorporated: a massive, fourteen-metre-wide tapestry in purple, red, green, yellow, orange and fawn, based on a paper cutout made by Utzon, hangs on the western wall of this room. The inspiration of the Great Barrier Reef is now made real.

These changes, of course, have not addressed any of the fundamental problems in the major and minor halls, but perhaps they are a small taste of things to come; the wheels of change are slow but they have begun to turn. In 2007 the building was finally given United Nations World Heritage listing, a move Utzon himself had championed for nearly a decade. Perhaps one day, a government of New South Wales will hold another international competition, calling for completion of the plans for the interiors and glass walls of the Sydney Opera House that Utzon began but was never allowed to finish. It may seem fanciful, but Sydney is a rich city, Australia a wealthy country, and the Sydney Opera House one of the world's great architectural wonders. The international excitement surrounding the refurbishment would be immense. Finally, a great artistic wrong could be righted.

ACKNOWLEDGEMENTS

All quotes from Jørn Utzon are from the June 1998 interview conducted by Daryl Dellora for the documentary film *The Edge of the Possible* and are used by kind permission of Film Art Doco Pty Ltd. Thanks also to Lin Utzon, who agreed to be interviewed for this story in August 2013. Other quotes are as follows: Patrick White (page 10) from *Flaws in the Glass: A Self-portrait*, Penguin, 1981; Utzon's letter of 28 February 1966 to Davis Hughes (pages 36–37), courtesy of the New South Wales Public Records Office; Ove Arup (page 53) and Peter Miller (pages 58–59), *The Masterpiece*, Philip Drew, Hardie Grant, 1999; Michael Lewis (page 55), *The Edge of the Possible*.

PENGUIN
SPECIALS

OTHER PENGUIN SPECIALS YOU COULD TRY:

Salad Days
Ronnie Scott

Beyond the Boom
John Edwards

Rudd, Gillard and Beyond
Troy Bramston

Is There No Place for Me?
Kate Richards

The Simple Life
Rhonda Hetzel

The Badlands
Paul French

What Would Gandhi Do?
Michael Kirby